marques vickers

OREGON COAST GUIDE:

BEAUTY, NOVELTY AND CURIOSITY

Oregon Coast Guide:
Beauty, Novelty and Curiosity

By Marques Vickers

**MARQUIS PUBLISHING
BAINBRIDGE ISLAND, WASHINGTON**

Version 1.3

Published by Marquis Publishing
InsiderSeriesBooks.com
Bainbridge Island, Washington

Vickers, Marques, 1957

Oregon Coast Guide:
Beauty, Novelty and Curiosity

Dedicated To My Two Daughters, Charline and Caroline

TABLE OF CONTENTS

PREFACE

Follow a picturesque adventure tour along the Oregon Coast's Interstate 101 that captures the majesty and quirkiness of the state. The 338-mile exploration begins at the California border in Brookings concluding with crossing the expansive Astoria-Megler Bridge into Washington. The background and commentary from each chapter is concise and insightful giving you an intimate glimpse of a West Coast region bountiful in aesthetics and generally absent of tourist herds. Ideal for the roadtrip warrior or day-tripper.

The routing omits sights and attractions that merit equal status as those profiled. The selection was wholly subjective by the author. Since my initial discovery in 2015, I have returned on numerous occasions, predominately during the winter months, to savor fresh attractions and a sparse visitor population. The Oregon Coast has been a remarkable discovery that never ceases to allure and consistently reveals a novel persona with each visit.

INSIDER SERIES BOOKS.com

Isaac Lee Patterson Bridge
Gold Beach to Wedderburn

The Isaac Lee Patterson Bridge, also known as the Rogue River Bridge is a concrete arch bridge than spans the Rogue River. The bridge extends Highway 101 at the point where the river empties into the Pacific Ocean, connecting the towns of Gold Beach and Wedderburm.

Completed in late 1931, the bridge posed numerous challenges during construction particularly concrete shrinkage. The ferry was officially opened earlier than expected on the day before Christmas due to damage sustained by the ferry *Rogue* from floodwaters. The bridge was officially dedicated in late May 1932. Designer Conde McCullough employed the Freyssinet method of pre-tensioning the arches during construction using hydraulic jacks. The bridge became the first usage of this technique in the United States. Traversing Oregon from the California border, the bridge becomes the initial introduction to McCullough, but certainly not the last.

The detailing of the bridge incorporates substantial Art Deco motifs, with prominent pylons at the ends, stepped Moderne elements and stylized Palladian windows crowned by sunbursts. The bridge is 1,898 feet long and consists of seven 230-foot deck arch spans and nine deck girder sections. The bridge was named after former Oregon Governor Isaac Lee Patterson.

Humbug Mountain
Near Port Orford

Twenty miles north of the Issac Lee Patterson Bridge is Humbug Mountain, one of the highest in Oregon. Dense foliage and drainage streams line the adjacent highway. The flora, fauna and overhanging moss create intoxicating viewing.

Humbug Mountain was christened its unusual moniker based on a perceived failure by Captain William Tichenor's exploration party of 1851. Tichenor's band of explorers veered north from their nearby settlement of Port Orchard instead of south due to the positioning of the mountain. Humbug rises 1,756 feet above sea level and juts out as a headland into the Pacific Ocean. The original Native Americans have labeled it various names including Sugarloaf, Mount Franklin and Metus. In matters of historical naming rights, their claims were historically overlooked. In matters of historical naming rights, their claims were historically overlooked..

INSIDER SERIES BOOKS.com

Battle Rock
Port Orford

Tichenor's name and questions regarding his competency would surface again further north regarding a land formation dubbed Battle Rock.

In 1850, the U.S. Congress passed the Oregon Donation Land Act that essentially transformed the Quatomah Native American tribe into squatters on their own historical lands. The tribe was neither obligated to sign the treaty nor contest its terms. Predictably, they determined nothing favorable to their interests in the language of the treaty.

Tichenor's expedition arrived the following year on the steamship Sea Gull and immediately established the initial American settlement at the base of Battle Rock. He stranded nine men from his ship and stocked them minimally. Their armaments including three aging flintlock muskets, a cache of rusty swords and a few pounds of ammunition. The men, clearly conscious of their vulnerability, managed to snatch a tiny signal gun and a four-pound cannon additionally from the ship.

The Quatomah leadership observed the proceedings and approached the intruders after their ship had departed. The tribe demanded that the group vacate immediately. The settlers had no means of escape and couldn't voluntarily leave. They constructed a shelter on the elevated seastack (Battle Rock) and huddled around their protective cannon.

Assuming the settler's intent to remain, a band of approximately one hundred Quatomahs attacked. The sole approach up to the camp was a narrow walkway. The cannon sufficiently dispersed the attackers upon its initial firing. The blast killed numerous approaching warriors and tossed many into the waters below.

Following the impact of the explosion, details become murky. Some accounts claim the outnumbered nine settlers repulsed the foes through hand-to-hand combat. Twenty-three natives were reportedly killed and two settlers wounded by arrows.

A fragile truce was reached when the settlers agreed to leave after 14 days, when their ship was due to return. The Quatomah respected the terms, but on the fifteenth day with no ship in sight, they renewed their attack. This time they doubled their force.

During the initial skirmish, the chief of the tribe was killed on the battlefield. The tribe briefly retreated, but set up a nearby camp with plans to obliterate the settlers the following day.

The doomed nine, sensing the impending end of their good fortune, evacuated northward in the dark. They traveled over a hundred miles amidst unfamiliar terrain into the Umpqua Valley with the Quatomah in pursuit. Their trek included wading through rivers and living on snails and wild berries. The story seems improbable since their pursuers knew the topography far better. It is unclear how they eventually found sanctuary. The historical narrative has each man surviving and relating his tales to an astonished and incredulous public. The party designated the fateful seastack formation Battle Rock.

In July 1851, Tichenor returned to Battle Rock with a well-armed regiment of seventy soldiers and officially established a settlement that he named Port Orford. Upon his retirement from the navy, Tichenor became a permanent resident and patriarch of the growing port that today remains a city of slightly over 1,000 residents. The historical narrative allows significant space for interpretation.

Bullards Bridge and Beach
Bandon

Bullards Bridge is a vertical-lift bridge, one of only two in Oregon, spanning the Coquille River near Bandon. It was completed in 1954 and replaced the Bullard Ferry service previously located approximately 80 feet upstream from the bridge. The lift span is flanked by two camelback truss spans and located adjacent east to Bullards Beach State Park. The name originates from the Bullard family, settlers of the region.

The bridge is visually unremarkable, but notable for several mishaps involving its original low overhead clearance. Following multiple instances of tall trucks striking the overhead girders, the construction was modified. In 2006, approximately two feet of height was added to accommodate the 9,000+ vehicles that cross daily.

Viewed to the northwest of the span, Bullards Beach hosts a diversity of beached tree trunks lining its shores. An accompanying campground fronts the Oregon Sand Dunes National Park featuring extended grassy fields and lowland forests.

Oregon Sand Dunes National Park
Coos River to Florence

The Oregon Sand Dunes stretches forty miles north from the Coos River in North Bend to the Siuslaw River in Florence along the coast. This territory comprises the largest expanse of coastal sand dunes in North America.

The most prominent feature of the dunes is their absence of exploitation and noticeable human intervention. The terrain is unspoiled and represents millions of years of wind and rain erosion. Some of the dunes elevate to 500 feet above sea level. Our ancestors viewed the identical beauty centuries before with the same sense of wonderment and appreciation.

Recreational opportunities are interspersed including off-road vehicle use, horseback riding, hiking trails and camping. Unlike so many natural wonders spoiled by the demands for amusement, these facilities wane into the background insignificant amidst the pristine elegance of nature's simplicity. Can one truly become blasé over such splendor?

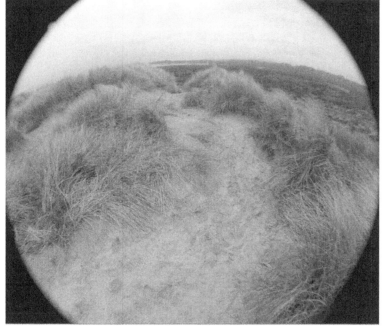

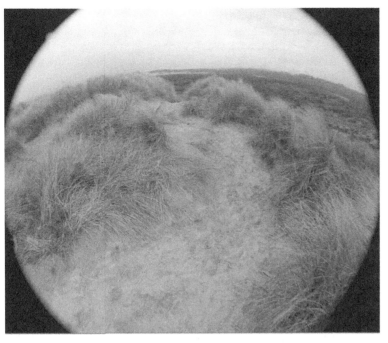

33

Conde McCullough Memorial Bridge
North Bend

The Conde B. McCullough Memorial Bridge is a cantilever bridge that spans Coos Bay on Interstate 101 near North Bend. When completed in 1936, it was originally named the Coos Bay Bridge. In 1947, it was renamed in honor of Conde McCullough following his untimely death the year before.

Ironically this bridge was one of the twelve along Interstate 101 credited to McCullough that he had minimal supervision over. During construction, he had taken a leave of absence to work on projects in Central America. Glenn S. Paxson became the acting State Bridge Engineer during his absence.

When completed, the bridge became Oregon's longest. The bridge features a concrete structure with steel sections. The main piers are supported on piles driven into the bay's bed. The main towers of the cantilever section were fabricated off-site and moved to the bridge in four sections.

The main span is 793 feet and overall length including the concrete approach is 5,305 feet. The main towers are 280 feet above the water surface, with curved sway bracing in a Gothic arch style. Pedestrian plazas meant to provide viewing points and access to the shoreline mark the ends of the bridge. The plazas are detailed with Art Moderne motifs.

INSIDER SERIES BOOKS.com

41

Spinreel Campground
North Bend

The Spinreel Campground is integrated into the center of the expansive dune park. The campground features sculpted elevating dunes with intervening water passages. It spreads over 1,000 acres of lands surrounded by forests. Near the campground entrance is a curious photographic composition of the Highway 101 overpass leap-frogging over a railroad bridge crossing adjacent Saunders Creek.

Umpqua River Bridge
Reedsport

The Umpqua River Bridge is a swing-span bridge crossing the Umpqua River in Reedsport. It is composed of a central swing span flanked by two reinforced concrete arches on each end. The swing span is employed to accommodate sailing vessels crossing underneath. This is the sole swing-span bridge remaining in the Oregon state highway system.

The span was designed by Conde McCullough and completed in 1936. The north end of the bridge is within Bolon Island Tideways State Scenic Corridor and the south extremity within the Reedsport city limits. An adjacent railroad bridge crosses the Umpqua to the east of the primary span.

Tahkenitch Creek
Gardiner

Continuing northward on Highway 101, Tahkenitch Creek
straddles both sides of the roadway with colorful wetlands
and marsh tide pools. Hiking is permissible into the denser
bordering forest and open sand dunes. The shoreline is
notable for its presence of black bears, raccoons, otter,
mink, deer and diverse varieties of shorebirds.

Cape Creek Bridge
Florence

Cape Creek Bridge is an arch bridge that spans Cape Creek along Highway 101 near Heceta Head. Opened in 1932, the bridge was designed by Conde McCullough and resembles a Roman aqueduct, with a single parabolic arch that spans half its length. The reinforced concrete construction is 619 feet long with a main span of 220 feet.

Heceta Head Lighthouse
Florence

In 1894, the Heceta Head lighthouse was constructed to assist navigating ships along the frequently treacherous Oregon coastline. The construction was completed merely six years after white settlers staked their claim of 164 acres of the surrounding land. The U.S. government purchased 19 acres within this territory to accommodate the lighthouse structure.

A noticeably absent party from this commercial transaction was the Siuslaw Native Americans who had populated the region for centuries, hunting sea lions, fishing and gathering sea bird eggs from the offshore rocks. The natives created a legend regarding the ocean cliffs in which *Animal People* constructed a great stone wall. The Animal People apparently tricked their Grizzly Bear brothers into falling to their deaths at that spot. There was no trickery involved in confiscating the Siuslaw lands...simply theft.

Spanish explorer Bruno de Heceta is credited with *discovering* the prominent rock formation during his notable late 18th century Pacific Northwest voyage. He was honored with naming rights.

The working lighthouse soars 205 feet above the ocean and is accessible by a walking trail. The structure measures 56-feet high. The adjoining lightkeeper's house has been restored and currently operates as a rustic inn. The lighthouse was renovated between 2011-2013 involving the replacement and restoration of the historic metalwork and masonry, windows and lens rotation mechanism. The Fresnel lens beam soars 21 miles out to sea and is considered the strongest light source on the Oregon coast.

The Pacific Ocean views from the Haceta cliffs are magnificent. They proved adequate compensation for a lighthouse operator's former solitary existence. A dual-level steel column bridge soars above the parking area as a reminder that contemporary highways have made the Oregon coast accessible to all.

Devil's Churn
Yachats

Devil's Churn is aptly named. The subterranean land formation is accessible by a descending stone stairway. Regardless of weather, its jagged rock base is a reminder of just who is in control of nature...no one.

The inlet was carved following thousands of years of wave actions shaping the basalt shoreline. The waves formed a deep-sea cavern whose roof eventually collapsed. The subsequent 100-foot crevice funnels momentous energy, as waves are compressed within. The ensuing spillage of spray and sea foam creates violent explosions and arbitrary hurling of water. The sequential drama of Devil's Churn resembles a vortex lashing out violently in all directions with the ferocity a whip's tail.

Sprays may vault thirty feet in height. Individuals securely fastened to overhanging ledges may discover themselves instantly drenched.

For those daring enough to navigate the walkway to its base, the turbulence is a worthy spectator performance. Debris is tossed and potential menace is a real threat. The impressive crown of Cape Perpetua, suspended 700 feet above the Churn, makes the descent into Hades particularly impressive. Avoid venturing into hell alone...unless you are a photographer with no better sense.

70

Seal Rock Wayside
Seal Rock

Seal Rock Wayside is an offshore formation popular with seals, sea lions, sea birds and accompanying marine life. The tide pools are popular for tourists and equally enjoyable sighting targets for amused birds. Three of the most prominent rocks are called Castle, Tourist and Elephant. They were privately purchased from the federal government in 1928.

Beaver Creek
Newport

Nearing the center of the Oregon Coastline and adjacent to Highway 101 is another enchanting waterway called Beaver Creek. A similarly named community is located significantly north in the state. This water body is a quaint meandering channel greeting motorists before their entry into the city of Newport via the Yaquina Bridge.

Yaquina Bay Bridge
Newport

The Yaquina Bay Bridge is an arch bridge spanning Yaquina Bay, south of Newport. Designed by Conde McCullough and opened in 1936, it superseded the final ferry crossing on Interstate 101. The project received funding from the United States Public Works Administration.

The 600-foot main span is a semi-through arch with the roadway penetrating the middle of the arch. It is flanked by 350-foot steel deck arches, with five concrete deck arches of diminishing size extending to the south landing. The main arch is distinctive by tall obelisk concrete finials on the main piers, with smaller decorative elements marking the ends of the flanking spans. The overall length of the bridge is 3,200 feet including concrete deck-girder approach spans.

The bridge employs Art Deco and Art Moderne design motifs and forms borrowed from Gothic architecture. Pedestrian viewing plazas augment the ends of the bridges.

83

Whale Bones Sculpture
Newport

One of the finest views of the Pacific Ocean currents may be savored on a Newport bluff above Nye Beach. Adjacent is a casted work created by local artist and poet Lon Brusselback featuring whale bones set at sharp perpendicular angles seemingly set in a natural resting position. Two accompanying stones feature engraved inscriptions, one from the Siletz Indians who once inhabited these shores.

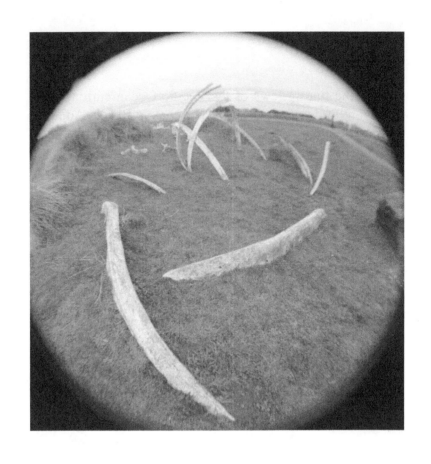

Devil's Punchbowl
Otter Rock

The Devil's Punchbowl differs from the Devil's Chasm primarily due to spectator access. Barricades prevent curious viewers from venturing too closely. The Punchbowl is speculated to have been created by two carved cave roofs eventually collapsing after centuries of ocean pounding. The hollowed out rock formation resembles a hefty shaped bowl vulnerable to the relentless incoming waves.

The center embraces a violent mix of churns, foams, and swirls creating the appearance of a witches brew. The outlying vistas are ideal for whale watching. Yellowish froth identified as whale sperm floats atop the wave's surface during the early months of winter.

93

94

Yaquina Head
Newport

Yaquina Head is a headland territory extending into the Pacific Ocean on the outskirts of Newport. The 100-acre territory features the Yaquina Bay Lighthouse atop a bluff at the mouth of the Yaquina River. Constructed in 1871, it is acknowledged to be the oldest structure in the region. It is also the only existing state lighthouse both constructed of wood and complete with living quarters attached.

The lighthouse was decommissioned in 1874 but restored to service in 1996. It operates a steady beam between dusk and dawn. The light originates from 161 feet above sea level.

103

Highway 101 Roadway Collapse
Moolack Beach

Just outside the city limits of Newport adjacent to Moolack Beach is a stretch of Interstate 101 that collapsed and remains in that state. The highway was long ago repaired and routes around the damage. The remnants are a fascinating glimpse of the potential abrupt destruction that might be triggered by a violent storm. Moolack Beach is approximately five miles long and named after the Chinook word for *elk*. Rooted petrified stumps that protrude from the beach are estimated to be 4,500 years old.

Namesake of a Forgotten Restaurant Chain
Lincoln City

In Santa Barbara, California the original Sambo's Restaurant opened in 1957. The beachfront restaurant offered a predictable, but generally agreeable menu. The décor featured seven paintings depicting scenes from Helen Bannermen's book *The Story of Little Black Sambo*. Over the course of the decade, the painting's original dark-skinned boy evolved into a light-skinned boy wearing a jeweled turban.

The story seemed incredulous then and even more ridiculous now. In summary, a young boy outsmarts four famished tigers, more interested in his colorful clothing than devouring him. The tigers chase each other around a tree attempting to snatch the desirable clothes until they turn into pancake batter. Sambo retrieves his clothing and his mother prepares him pancakes from the batter for breakfast. This narrative for those actually familiar with the story probably stimulated few appetites for pancakes and the mere notion of dining on four tigers seems indigestible.

Unless you have resided in an isolated cavern in a remote continent in excess of the past century, you may be unaware that the term *Sambo*, (even dating back to the 1500s), has assumed a degrading and derogatory racist connotation. The original Santa Barbara restaurant claims the Sambo's name was apparently constructed from portions of the original two founder's names. The connection with Bannerman's story evolved later via their coincidental choices in décor. The restaurant became an immediate success from the outset.

The Sambo's restaurant chain expanded and flourished during the 1970s, ultimately peaking with 1,117 locations nationwide. The company was a pioneer in offering profit sharing to restaurant managers. This attractive incentive proved popular stimulating explosive growth. Within a decade, the corporate financial foundation eroded and in 1981, the company declared bankruptcy.

From the outset of their national expansion, the Sambo's name proved problematic. Headquarter management experimented with renaming and re-branding alternatives. These efforts proved futile. Rapid financial hemorrhaging made reinvention impossible. By October 1984, all of the restaurant outlets had either been shuttered or were sold to competitors...with a single exception.

The original Santa Barbara outlet continues to operate in a cultural time warp, serving daily breakfast and lunch as they have since their 1957 opening.

That identical year, a privately owned Lil' Sambo's Family Restaurant opened in Lincoln City. Due to the coincidental timing, it is unavoidable to speculate as to whether there has been any prior association with the defunct Sambo's chain.

The Lincoln City restaurant addresses the query on their website:

One question we are often asked is whether or not we were ever part of the Sambo's national chain. The answer is no. Our name is borrowed from the hero of a fictional story about an Indian boy, tigers, and pancakes written by Helen Bannerman in 1899. The words *Black Sambo* however is judiciously absent from their explanation and restaurant signage.

Neskowin Beach
Neskowin

The Cascade headland of Neskowin is frequently deserted and pristine. The adjoining town is quaint and tourist accommodating. The exposed cove is superior entertainment. Viewing the sun lower between the ideally positioned seastacks is a reminder that no fabricated amusement park can ever adequately replicate the majesty of nature. There are three stunning nearby on Cascade Head. They included one crossing Knight's Park, another through the Siuslaw National Forest and the third elevates through a Sitka Spruce-Western Hemlock rain forest. Chitwood Falls cascade off the backside cliff at Hart's Cove.

Sand Lake Recreation Area
Sand Lake

As Highway 101 veers inland towards Tillamook, a coastal routed Resort Drive heads west into Pacific City. From Pacific City, follow the northbound Cape Kiwanda Drive that eventually becomes Sandlake Road. The routing passes both the Sand Lake and Sandlake Creek water bodies before bordering over a thousand acres of open sand dunes, surrounded by forests and adjacent to the Pacific Ocean. The dunes extend to the northeast approximately four miles.

113

Storm Rock and Three Arch Rocks National Wildlife Refuge
Oceanside

Further northwest from Sandlake Road, Cape Lookout Road traces the coastline until it reaches a park by that name. The road then becomes Whiskey Creek Road continuing along the Netarts Bay estuary complete with picturesque water channels. Continuing north to Oceanside, Storm Rock and the Three Arch Rocks National Wildlife Refuge are located a half-mile off the coast. The Three Arch Rocks consists of 15 acres on three large and six small rocky islands. President Theodore Roosevelt established the refuge in 1901 because it featured the largest colony of breeding tufted puffins and largest common murre colony south of Alaska. It is the only known northern Oregon pupping site for the Steller sea lion.

INSIDER SERIES BOOKS.com

Cape Meares Lighthouse
Tillamook

Constructed in 1890, the Cape Meares Lighthouse served as the station for Tillamook Bay. The original structure included two keeper's houses, two oil houses and two cisterns. A workroom and garage were later added. In 1963, the lighthouse was deactivated and replaced by a newer tower. During a stretch of inactivity and abandonment, vandalism resulted in the keeper's quarters being demolished and four of the bulls-eyes in the Fresnel lens being stolen. The lighthouse projects illumination visible for 21 miles.

INSIDER SERIES BOOKS.com

Octopus Tree
Tillamook

Lodged within the adjacent forest lands of the Cape Meares Lighthouse, an enormous and mysterious Sitka spruce branches out in an unusual candelabra shape. Estimated to be nearly 300-years old, the tree's massive limbs extend like tentacles from the base resulting in its designation as *Octopus Tree*. The legend surrounding its unusual appearance speculates that the branches were forced into a horizontal position while still young and flexible. Each was ultimately released to grow vertically giving the tentacle appearance of slithering away from the base trunk. This ceremonial tree may have been employed to hold objects such as canoes or corpses for ritualistic purposes. In the distance, whales may be sighted above the surf during spawning season.

INSIDER SERIES BOOKS.com

Tillamook Creamery
Tillamook

Returning back to Highway 101 following the coastal diversion, the Tillamook Creamery is the headquarters facility of an enormous dairy cooperative. The cooperative features nearly 100 regional dairy farms and is renowned for their cheese, ice cream, butter, sour cream and yogurt products distributed nationally. The visitor's center was architecturally designed to resemble a contemporary barn featuring enormous windows streaming in natural daylight. The facility hosts over one million visitors annually featuring a self-guided tour with video presentations and interactive kiosks. Visitors are instructed regarding the cheese making process, cheese packaging process and the ice-cream production process from a viewing gallery over the main production floor.

INSIDER SERIES BOOKS.com

The Fish Peddler
Bay City

Mountains of stacked oyster shells front an extended peer that leads to an oyster processing plant where the local mollusks are shell, packaged and distributed to restaurants and grocery chains. A restaurant and distribution warehouse further down the pier accommodate visitors and buyers, yet it remains the stacked shells that capture driver's attention and the legion of seagulls that crown the top of the pile.

Oregon Coast Scenic Railroad
Garibaldi

A historic Heisler type steam locomotive pulls tourist trains along the coast between Garibaldi and Wheeler. For over a century these trains hauled lumber down the tortuous grades of the coast rails to the mills of Tillamook along with goods to the community. During the summer and autumn tourists has become the transportable cargo.

Haystack Rock
Cannon Beach

The monolithic sea stack measures 235 feet high rising from Cannon Beach and accessible by foot at low tide. The rock's tide pools support many intertidal animals including starfish, sea anemone, crabs, chitons, limpets and sea slugs. The surface is a nesting site for numerous sea birds, including terns and puffins. Composed of basalt, Haystack Rocks was formed by lava flows emanating from the Blue Mountains and Columbia basin an estimated 15-16 million years ago.

Seaside Carousel Mall
Seaside

The settlement of Seaside was established in 1806 by a group of participants from the Lewis and Clark Expedition. They constructed a salt-making cairn on the site. The actual community would not be incorporated until 1899 and become a prominent summer tourist destination. The beach and half-mile promenade are the two most visible attractions. The third is located at the middle of Broadway Street, the downtown main shopping district. A children's carousel operates daily in the center of a 20-store boutique shopping mall.

INSIDER SERIES BOOKS.com

Astoria's Historic Hauntings
Astoria

Astoria was founded in 1811 making it both the first American settlement west of the Rocky Mountains and the oldest city in Oregon. The town rests strategically on the south shore of the Columbia River at the juncture where it flows into the Pacific Ocean. The city was named for John Jacob Astor, a New York City entrepreneur whose American Fur Company founded Fort Astoria and monopolized the fur trade during the early 19th century.

Astoria became a significant Pacific seaport and trading center ultimately eclipsed by Portland and Seattle. Shipwrecks, Shanghai tunnels, unexplained deaths and rampant vice tainted the community with a notorious reputation. Astoria was labeled the *Graveyard of the Pacific*. Lumber, fishing and fish processing sustained the local economy. In 1945, thirty canneries lined its shoreline.

The downtown historic district endured a devastating December 1922 fire destroying thirty-six blocks of hotels, saloons, boarding houses, professional and retail establishments. Masonry and more durable materials replaced the former structures, compised primarily of wood. Many were completed within two years following the devastation. Today, the lumber industry has long vanished, shipwrecks have become rare and the canneries that once lined the port demolished. The population has steadied to approximately 9,000 presuming we are counting living souls.

Paranormal activity has been recorded throughout various

local landmarks. Given Astoria's infamous reputation and ill-fortuned past, spirits and hauntings should be presumed. The Shanghai tunnel network located beneath downtown would be an ideal starting point to register such activity if they were readily accessible. Drugged ship crewmembers were forced through these tunnels into undesirable serfdom. The process was involuntary and frequently violent.

Amongst the most commonly cited above ground locations for psychic abnormalities include:

Captain George Flavel Mansion and Daughter's Residence Constructed in 1885 in the Queen Anne architectural style at 441 8th Street, the Captain George Flavel Mansion remains a jeweled showpiece of design and taste. Flavel was a renowned Columbia River maritime pilot and one of Astoria's first millionaires. The mansion remained inhabited by the family until 1934 when the property was ceded to the city. The gift was tepidly received and there was even an ungracious attempt to return it back to the family. By 1951, there was political discussion regarding demolition. Concerned citizens intervened and were able to raise sufficient funding to construct proper renovation. The building was ultimately converted into a local history museum. The Captain and his wife are rumored to still passively roam the property during their infinite idle hours.

A more intriguing Flavel family residence is located at 627 15th Street. Constructed in 1901 in the Colonial Revival style, the 4,644-square mansion was inhabited by Captain Flavel's daughter and unmarried grandchildren Harry Sherman and Mary Louise. Throughout their lives, the trio exhibited a unique perspective regarding *family values*.

In 1947, Harry reportedly locked his mother inside a room that he was guarding with a hatchet. A water utility worker responded to her persistent screaming. Teenager Harry wounded the intruder earning him the nickname *Hatchet Harry*. The incident colored debate regarding the status of his sanity. Both his mother and sister defended him at trial emphasizing an overreaction by the utility worker.

Harry, Florence and Mary would inhabit the steadily decaying property until 1990. The trio abruptly fled following Harry's stabbing of a neighbor and his being declared guilty at trial. The residence remained stagnant, derelict and abandoned with garbage cluttered everywhere inside. The trio had accumulated nearly a century of hoarded refuse.

A perception of the family's cheapness was magnified when Harry made headlines soon afterwards in Pennsylvania. He was arrested for stealing towels from a hotel. He fled, but was ultimately captured by the FBI who extradited him back to Astoria for his earlier conviction. He simmered in jail for a year awaiting trial, was then released, and returned to Massachusetts to awaiting tragedy. During his absence, his mother had died at the University of Massachusetts Medical Center. Neither child would pick up Florence's body from the morgue for burial. Henry and Mary merely returned back to Oregon and began living in the Beaverton area.

Harry would die in 2010, but history would repeat as his body remained in the morgue for nine months because his sister refused to pay for a funeral. He was buried in a graveyard for indigents field in the Portland area.

Their former Astoria residence continued to slide into decline and local political dispute over accumulating unpaid taxes. Consistently the Flavel trio had simply dodged responsibility. Finally a compromise was reached between Mary and the city of Astoria. The building was showcased and auctioned to the highest bidder in 2015. The winning bidder sagely noted that it might require the rest of his life to properly restore the property. His vision proved prophetic. He died in 2018 from multiple myeloma cancer approximately one month before he had planned to actually move in.

Mary Louise died on October 20, 2018 at the age of 93 in a nursing home concluding a family legacy of curiosity, gossip and dodging community responsibility. Reports of ghosts and haunting could simply have been prompted by the state of the mansion's decay. However factoring in the family's tortured history, paranormal activity would seem *normal*.

Liberty Theatre
The theater opened in 1925 hosting vaudeville acts and cinema symbolizing the city's rebirth following the downtown fire three years earlier. Designed in the Italian Renaissance style, the auditorium features a series of 12 mural-style paintings depicting Venetian canal scenes accentuating a Mediterranean atmosphere.

An apparition of a suave gentleman attired in a tuxedo is dubbed *Handsome Paul*. He is rumored to occupy the building along with an accompanying elderly female. The partners in mischief have been accused of turning on the soda fountains and popcorn machines during the shuttered late hours. Other reported phenomena have included objects moving mysteriously, doorknobs rattling and erratic door knockings.

Doll Asylum House
A 1906 Victorian residence located at 1188 Harrison Avenue blends seamlessly into the sloping neighborhood. From an outside view, nothing appears unusual. The exterior painted skin is immaculate. If Astoria has become a magnet for spirits due to its tortured history, the staged interior *Doll Asylum* on Harrison Avenue is a Dreamcatcher of potential nightmares

Within the interior, a collection in excess of 1,200 children's toys and dolls has been purposely staged into scenes described as *horrific* and *humorous*. The inspiration stemmed from the resident couple's obsession with Halloween by interpretive design. The displays are promoted for visitation during seasonal festivities. Spectators have reported no specific hauntings other than intrusive and disturbing images invading their nightly slumber.

CLATSOP COUNTY HISTORICAL SOCIETY

FLAVEL HOUSE
- MUSEUM -

Built for Captain George Flavel, 1885

Astoria-Megler Bridge
Astoria to Megler, Washington

The Astoria-Megler Bridge is a steel cantilever through truss bridge spanning the Columbia River and connecting the states of Oregon and Washington. Constructed in 1966, the four-mile bridge is the longest continuous truss bridge in North America and became the final segment of U.S. Interstate Route 101.

Ferry service between the two states began in 1926 and the operation was purchased by the Oregon Department of Transportation in 1946. The typical crossing required over a half-hour and did not operated during inclement weather. The bridge was designed by William Adair Bugge and required four years of construction. The construction costs were financed by tolls until they were removed in 1993, two years ahead of schedule.

Approximately 8,000 vehicles and bicycles cross the bridge daily and during one day in October, pedestrians are allowed to cross during the *Great Columbia Crossing*. The bridge features 8 main spans and 33 approach spans. The width is 28 feet.

INSIDER SERIES BOOKS.com

Author, photographer and visual artist Marques Vickers was born in 1957 in Vallejo, California. He graduated from Azusa Pacific University in Los Angeles and became the Public Relations and Executive Director for the Burbank, California Chamber of Commerce between 1979-84.

Professionally, he has operated travel, apparel, wine, rare book and publishing businesses. His paintings and sculptures have been exhibited in art galleries, private collections and museums in the United States and Europe. He has previously lived in the Burgundy and Languedoc regions of France and currently lives in the South Puget Sound region of Western Washington.

He has written and published over one hundred and forty books spanning a diverse variety of subjects including true crime, international travel, social satire, wine production, architecture, history, fiction, auctions, fine art, poetry and photojournalism.

He has two daughters, Charline and Caroline who reside in Europe.

Made in the USA
Coppell, TX
26 February 2025

46434351R00090